# Friends

## A Handbook About Getting Along Together

by Sandra Ziegler
illustrated by Seymour Fleishman

Distributed by Standard Publishing,
Cincinnati, Ohio 45231.

THE CHILD'S WORLD

ELGIN, ILLINOIS 60120

Distributed by Standard Publishing, 8121 Hamilton Avenue,
Cincinnati, Ohio 45231.

Library of Congress Cataloging in Publication Data

Ziegler, Sandra.
    Friends, a handbook about getting along together.

    (Living the good life)
    SUMMARY: Explores what it means to have and be
friends and what it is like to be friends with God.
    1. Friendship—Juvenile literature.    2. Children—
Religious life.    [1. Friendship.    2. Conduct of life.
3. Christian life]    I. Fleishman, Seymour.
II. Title.    III. Series.
BJ1533.F8Z53        241'.676        80-17529
ISBN 0-89565-174-2

# Friends

**A Handbook About Getting Along Together**

# About *Friends*

*Friends* is a handbook about getting along with other people. It is one of a series of books entitled "Living the Good Life."

In this book, many aspects of friendship are discussed. These include:
- what a friend is,
- why people want friends,
- the kinds of people who make good friends,
- how to be a friend,
- the variety of people who can be friends,
- what friends can expect of each other.

This book can be used at church or at home. Students can read it to themselves or to each other; or the book can be read, a little at a time, to or with younger children. Children can think and talk about the ideas and examples given in the book.

Children need and want friends. This book, *Friends,* will help them think about friendship and how to make and keep good friends.

# CONTENTS

Do you have a friend?

If you are like most people, you probably said yes. Almost all of us are friends with someone.

Did you ever wonder why?

Why is it so important to have a friend? Or to be a friend? Why can't each of us just go it alone?

Maybe this whole idea of friends is something to kick out of the way like a rusty tin can.

Maybe it isn't.

Read on. See what you think.

# CHAPTER 1

## What Is a Friend?

A friend is someone special. He is someone you know very well. He knows you too. You call each other by name. When you see each other, you wave and call, "Hello."

Bill went to visit Grandma. They went to a shopping center. Grandma bought Bill an ice cream cone. Then she wanted to go into the hardware store. Bill said, "You go, Grandma, I will wait here until I finish my ice cream."

Bill did not see any friends in the shopping center. All the people were strangers to Bill. A friend has to be someone you know.

You can be friends with many people at the same time. You can be friends in one way with one person. You can be friends in another way with another person. But everyone you make friends with, knows you. And you know them.

You can be friends with. . .

your mother. . .

your father. . .

your sister. . .

and your brother.

You can be friends with
the neighbors,
a teacher,
the preacher.

Even an animal can be your friend, in his own
special way.

A friend is someone who likes you.

You can know someone's name. You can know what house he lives in. You can even know the color of his bicycle. Still you might not know him well enough to be his friend.

Just knowing is not enough. You have to know someone well enough to feel something. That something you have to feel is. . .

What makes you like someone you know
enough to become a friend?

Being alike helps!

Friends are usually about the same age. Girls tend to have more friends who are girls. Boys tend to have more friends who are boys. Girls and boys, however, often are friends when they are interested in the same things. Friends often live in the same neighborhood. They may even go to the same church,
or club,
or school,
or park.

Liking the same things helps too.

People who like each other enough to become friends usually like the same things: skating, fishing, games, church activities, for instance.

And they think sharing together makes doing these things even more fun.

Two children who like each other enough to be "best friends" have fun just being together.

That's really liking!

Friends who have good times just being together really care about each other. They care about each other the way Prince Jonathan cared about his friend—David, the shepherd.

(If you don't know this story, you may read it in 1 Samuel 18: 1-4; 19: 1-7; 20; 2 Samuel 9.)

*A friend loves at all times*
*(from Proverbs 17: 17).*

A friend is someone you trust and who trusts you.

Did you ever know someone you couldn't trust—the kind of person who made you want to chain up your bicycle and hide your piggy bank?

A friend has to be someone you can trust. Do you know why? One of the most important things friends do together is tell each other things, such as how they feel, or what they think.

Imagine having a friend who shouted all the special secret things you told him through a megaphone for everyone to hear. No one would like that. No, you have to be able to trust your friends.

Now you know what a friend is. Maybe you can't draw a picture of one yet. But you know a friend is:

- Someone who knows you.

- Someone you know.

- Someone who likes you.

- Someone you like.

- Someone who trusts you.

- Someone you trust.

Now you are ready to ask the next question. . .

# CHAPTER 2

## Why Would I Want a Friend?

Some things you can do best all by yourself:

reading

praying

writing

painting

Trying to do it alone is much harder if you want to:

teeter-totter

play a baseball game

or swim in a buddy-system pool.

Sometimes it is good to be alone.

Sometimes it is better to be with a friend.

One is not right, and the other wrong. Both are good and you can choose.

A friend is for when being alone will not do.

A friend is someone to share with.

You can share

- what you like,
- places you like,
- what you believe,
- how you think, and how you feel.

A friend is also a helper.

You help your friend, and your friend helps you.

A friend is someone who cares.

You care about him, and he cares about you.

A friend believes in you.

He believes you will be the one to win the all-school race.

You believe that your friend can be counted on to keep the promises he makes.

A friend is someone to do something with. . .

...not just big things, such as seeing the circus, but little things, such as skipping stones and counting birds.

Friends are special. A friend is:

- Someone who can keep you from being alone when you don't want to be alone.
- Someone who will leave you alone when you do want to be alone.
- Someone who will understand your good and not-so-good feelings.

And best of all, if your friend is a Christian friend, you can share what is most important to both of you—your faith. It's nice to know God takes care of both you and your friend.

# CHAPTER 3

## What Kind of Person Makes a Good Friend?

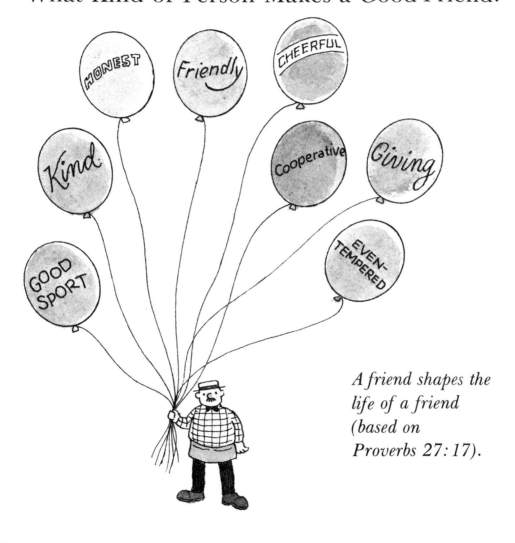

*A friend shapes the life of a friend (based on Proverbs 27:17).*

Did you ever know someone who could step out into a hailstorm and say, "Isn't this a beautiful day?" and mean it? He could even make you agree! Right while the stones were pounding your head!

Some children are like that. . .cheerful. They seldom get down in the dumps. Oh, everyone does that now and then. But a cheerful child spreads cheerfulness. It's great to have a cheerful person for your friend.

Some boys and girls find it easy to make friends with new children at school or in the neighborhood. Such a child is friendly to others. He doesn't wait for them to make the first move.

The Bible says:

*A man who has friends must show himself friendly (from Proverbs 18: 24).*

It's true, don't you think? Wouldn't you rather be friendly to someone who is friendly to you?

If you want lots of friends, the way to make them is to be friendly.

Once a storekeeper said, "Honesty is the best policy." He meant: I cannot lie, or steal, or cheat my customers. If I do, no one will buy at my store. He was probably right.

Among friends, being honest is the only way to be.

If your friend steals your flashlight, how do you feel? Angry, of course. You say, "I'm not going to be friends with him anymore!"

If you told him a lie, he would say the same thing about you.

You can't be a friend to someone unless you are honest with him.

Could you be friends with someone who stomped home if he didn't get his own way?

I know your answer. No. You can't be friends with someone who will never cooperate, someone who always wants his own way.

That's just not how friends treat each other.

Sharon is always the first one on the block to get every new toy. Her brother Sammy gets them too. They have a wonderful house in the backyard. It is so big that it has a door you can walk through standing up. Their Daddy made it. The sink inside has running water if you fill the bucket outside. The electric lights work. You can even bake a little cake in the tiny oven.

Sharon and Sammy are always giving. They say, "Let's play at our house."

Sharon and Sammy are good friends!

Merle is kind to everyone. He helps little children to cross the street. He carries groceries for old people. If you have to do yard work before you can play, Merle will help you.

It's easy to be Merle's friend.

It isn't always so easy to be Albert's friend. Sometimes Albert doesn't pay attention to what he's doing. Once when he was at Jimmy's house, he almost let Jimmy's parakeet out of the cage when the window was open.

It sure is a good thing Gus was there. Gus always keeps his cool. He keeps us all calm.

We're lucky to have Gus as a friend.

In fact, when your friends are as different as Albert and Gus and Jimmy, you learn something that really matters! THE FRIENDS YOU CHOOSE CAN CHANGE THE WAY YOU ARE!

If your friends cause trouble, you keep getting into jams. If your friends are good kids and stay out of mischief, you will stay out of scrapes too.

Think about it! That's why it's so important to choose the kind of people that make the best friends.

Remember Albert, the one who doesn't pay attention? Well, Albert wins the award for "good sport." It's true that he is the one most likely to make a touchdown for the wrong team because he ran the wrong way. But if he did, Albert would be the first to congratulate the winner.

Even when he lost.

Albert is a good sport, and he plays by the rules. I guess that is why, in spite of everything, we all like Albert. . . and call him friend.

So. . .

What kind of person do you have to be to be a
good friend?

Giving like Sharon?

And kind like Merle?

And calm like Gus?

And a good sport like Albert?

And honest? And cheerful?

And cooperative? And friendly?

All at once?

Do you have to be the salesman with the most balloons?

Of course not!

But think about that salesman for a minute. The more balloons he has, the more choice you have when buying one. Of course, if he has lost a balloon or two, you still have plenty to choose from. You can still get a good balloon, a colorful one, one that is fun to have.

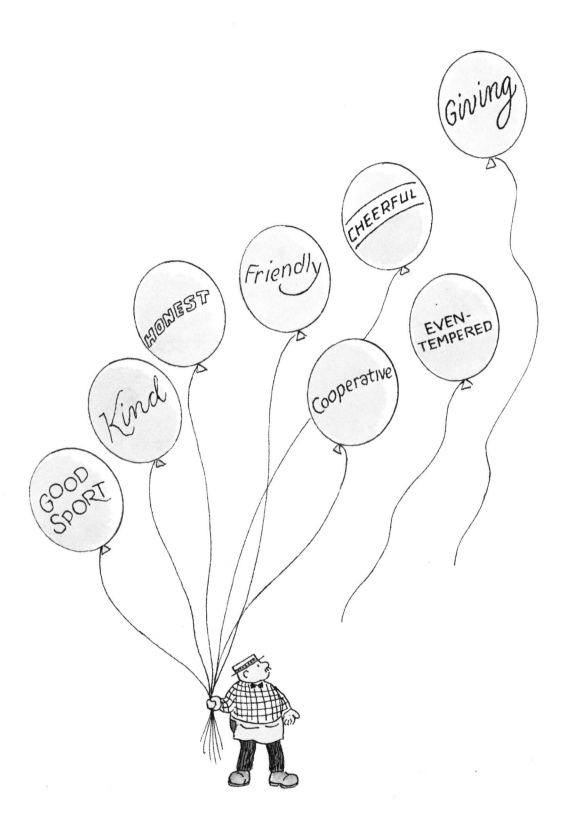

On the other hand, if the salesman is down to one balloon, he may want to get some more.

Now think about choosing a good friend. Wouldn't you rather have a friend who has lots of good qualities? If someone has only one good quality, not many will pick him for a close friend. He needs to develop other good qualities.

How many of the following qualities do you have? Are you. . .

- kind?

- honest?

- friendly?

- cheerful?

- generous?

- a good sport?

- even-tempered?

- cooperative?

*There is a friend that sticks closer than a brother ( from Proverbs 18:24).*

# CHAPTER 4

## How Can I Be a Friend?

If you want to be a friend, do you know how to start? You can start by making a friend. A good way to do that is to smile at someone.

A smile says you want to be friendly.

A person who is smiled at feels good. He thinks, there is someone nice. He likes me. He might want to be my friend. I might like to know him.

So he does something very special. He smiles back.

This doesn't happen just at play. It can happen anywhere—even in a department store. You smile. She smiles back.

You answer a returned smile with some words of greeting.

When you begin to talk, you take another important step in friendship.

Talking is important. So is listening.

When friends talk and listen to each other, they get to know some heavy stuff about each other. They ask and answer questions such as the following.

- Who are you?
- What kind of person are you?
- How do you feel about things?
- What do you want to be?
- What do you want to do?
- What do you like?
- What do you hate?

When you were little, and a friend came over to play, he played his way and you played your way. You played side by side. But you played alone.

Now you are big, and you and your friends can really play together. Playing together is important in friendship.

Don't just sit there—wishing. Get up. Join the group. Play with them.

Nobody has all the ideas in the world. That's why friends share ideas. One child thinks of something to do. He says, "Let's do it!"

Someone else has an idea. He says, "O.K. we could. . ."

More and more ideas come.

To be a good friend, tell your playmates when you get an idea. Maybe they won't think of it. If you don't tell your idea, all of you will miss the fun.

Of course, sometimes there are arguments when people play together. What does a friend do then? What should you do then? Fight as these girls are doing? Or "pick up your bat and go home"?

Fighting is not the answer. And anybody can pick up his bat and go home. Someone who wants to be friends should stay and try to work it out. To work out the problem, try calm talking and more calm talking.

Here are some other good thoughts about getting along with others.

Make friends, not war

A soft answer turns away anger.

I NEVER MET A PERSON I DIDN'T LIKE.

VOTE FOR FRIENDSHIP!

Do you know what the nicest compliment is?
It is, "Will you help me?"

It says:

- I like you.
- I think you're smart.
- Maybe you know something I don't. Maybe I could learn from you.
- Let's share.
- Do you want to be friends?
- We could be buddies.

Friends don't just share the fun things. They share the work things too!

Friends say, "We should clean our classroom."

"Let's do it together."

"Working together is easier than working alone."

"We could bring our lunch and have a party when we're done."

"Let's do what needs doing, together."

Now you know what to do to be a friend:

- Smile your friendly smile.
- Talk to people you meet.
- Be a good listener.
- Join the group and play together.
- Tell your ideas to your friends.
- Try to get along with others.
- Ask you friends to help you.
- Do things together.

Did you discover that what you should do to be a friend is what you would like your friends to do? You have discovered, *The Golden Rule.*

If you don't know it, you can read it in Matthew 7: 12.

# CHAPTER 5

## Will All My Friends Be Children?

Now you know what a friend is. You know there are some good reasons to have friends. You know it's important to choose the right friends. You even know what kinds of people make good friends, and how to be a friend yourself.

What do you think? Will all your friends be children?  Of course not!  Friends can be any age.  Or any size.

It is not how a person looks. It is how a person acts that makes him a friend.

God is a friend.

God doesn't speak to us face to face. But He listens. He hears our prayers. He speaks to us from the Bible. He loves us. If we love and obey Him, we can be friends with God, because He understands and cares about us.

Mother cares about you. She wants to share how you feel and what you think. Because she is your friend, she will help you. She always will love you, no matter what. As a good friend, Mother is always there.

You and Father are friends. You share things
with each other. Father really cares about you,
just as Mother does. That's what friendship is:
loving and caring for someone.

Older brothers and sisters are friends too. They help you learn to fix the chain on your bike. Or they teach you how to fix your hair. Sometimes you go places together. Or you just find time to talk about things. Big sisters and brothers make special friends. Usually they are forever friends. They don't move away and forget you the way other friends sometimes do.

You will probably think of others, older than you are, who are your friends. Find a tablet and pencil. Make a list of all the older friends you think of. . .

Grandpa,

Grandma,

Coach Jones,

Miss Miller, at the library,

My teacher. . .

How long is your list?

Jesus knew about how friends treat each other. He told a story about friends. Does the picture help you remember? Can you tell the story? If you want to read the story Jesus told, you will find it in Luke 11: 5-13.

# CHAPTER 6

## What Will My Friends Expect of Me?

A gardener expects his prize-winning roses to be perfect.

That's what your mother expects of the pie that she bakes to take to the county fair.

Being perfect is not something you can expect from a friend. A friend cannot expect it from you either. A machine might be perfect. People seldom are.

There are some things you can expect from a friend. He will expect the same from you too.

Hurry on to find out what those things are.

"Do you want to go horseback riding tomorrow?" Dave asked.

"No," said Ken. "I have to go to the dentist over in Cedarville."

Dave believed Ken. He knew his friend was always honest. He did not have to stop at Ken's and check on him. Ken knew Dave would believe him. He never lied to Dave. They were always honest with each other.

Bob and Danny are good friends. They share many activities. One thing they share is an interest in plants. They think the plant food they use is almost a magic ingredient. It makes the plant leaves green. It helps the plants grow.

Sharing is a magic ingredient too. It makes friendship grow. Sharing so many things helps Bob and Danny to be close friends.

When Mary and Kathy got to the school door, Mary held it open. "Thank you," said Kathy.

Mary dropped her fork at lunch. Kathy picked it up. "Thank you," said Mary.

Mary and Kathy have good manners. They use them with each other. People who are polite to each other are better friends. That's because the most important part of being polite is being kind and thoughtful.

Bert and Terry are good friends who are into computers. They are playing a computer game with Jack and Kevin.

When Bert went to get a drink, Jack said, "Bert will never win. He's not good enough!"

"Oh, yes, he will," said Terry. "Bert's smart." Terry is loyal to Bert. Bert is also loyal to Terry.

That's why they are such good friends.

Bert and Terry respect each other. They are always loyal to each other.

Do you expect your friends to respect you? To be loyal?

What do you think? Should friends support each other? Do you support your friends? Do they support you?

Let's suppose Becky is your good friend. She runs for office in the class election. Do you try to get others to vote for her?

Lara calls Krissy on the telephone. Krissy seldom says, "I don't have time to talk." She might, though, if she had something very important to do. And Lara would understand.

Usually Krissy takes time to talk to Lara.

Friendships take time. People who really want to be friends make time for them.

There sure is a lot to remember about getting along with others! So let's make it easy. Hang these three posters in your memory, and you will be close to doing it all right!

Having friends. . .

That's not an idea to kick out of the way like a rusty tin can. Don't you agree?

And in closing, let's remember—wherever we go, whatever we do, our best friend is Jesus!